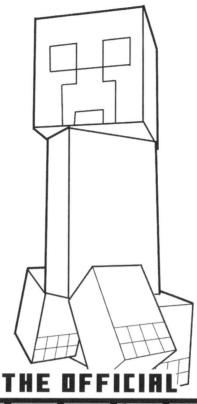

# THE OFFICIAL
# MINECRAFT
# COLOURING ADVENTURE BOOK

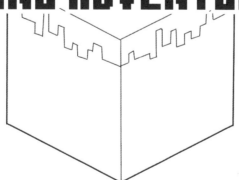

**Titan**
BOOKS

LONDON

# HELLO FRIEND!

This book is yours to show off the awesome creativity that you have gained while mining, building and exploring Minecraft's wide and wonderful worlds. Throughout the pages of this official Minecraft colouring book, you will use that same creativity and sense of adventure to colour some of the mobs, places, and situations you have experienced on your travels – and turn them into your own works of art! With scenes including Alex and Steve facing a horde of creepers and a ghast-haunted Nether panorama, you can use your weapon of choice – coloured pencils, crayons, markers – and your imagination to create something amazing! Now, go forth and colour without limits!

Have Fun!

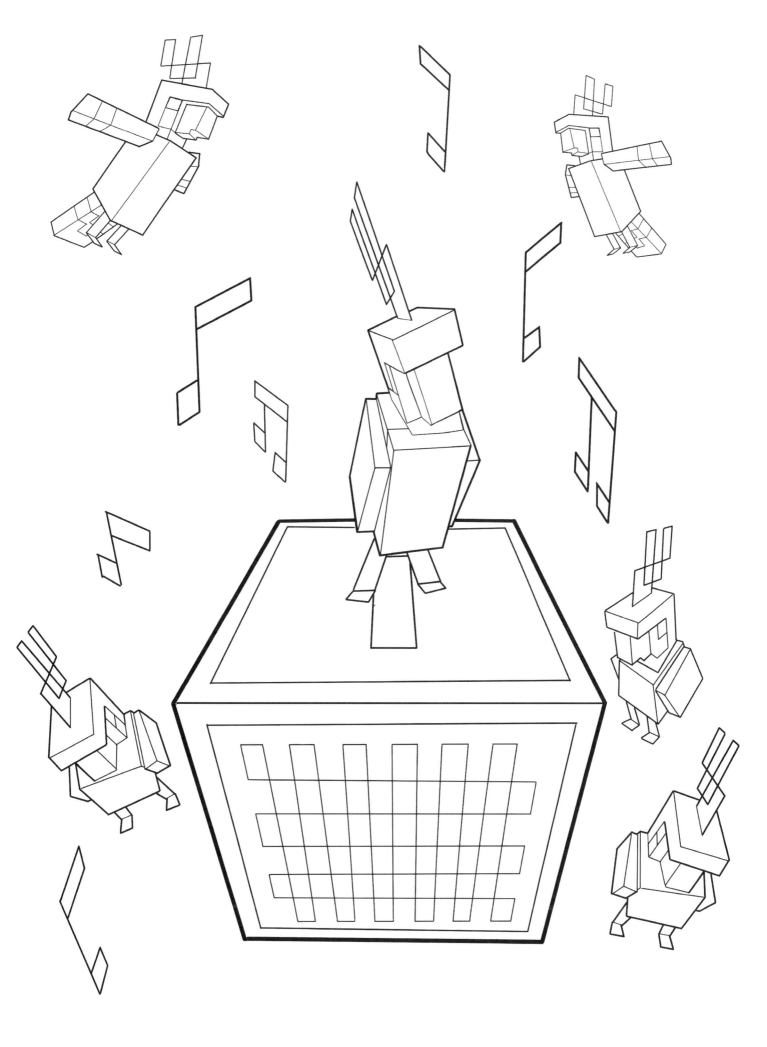

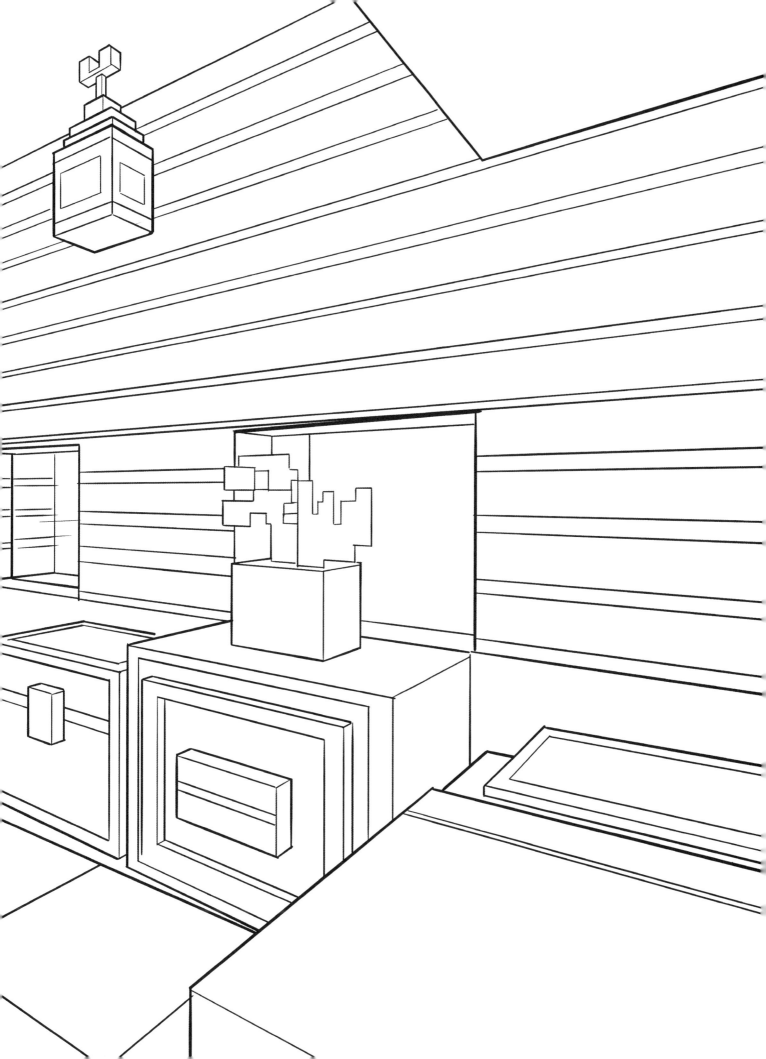

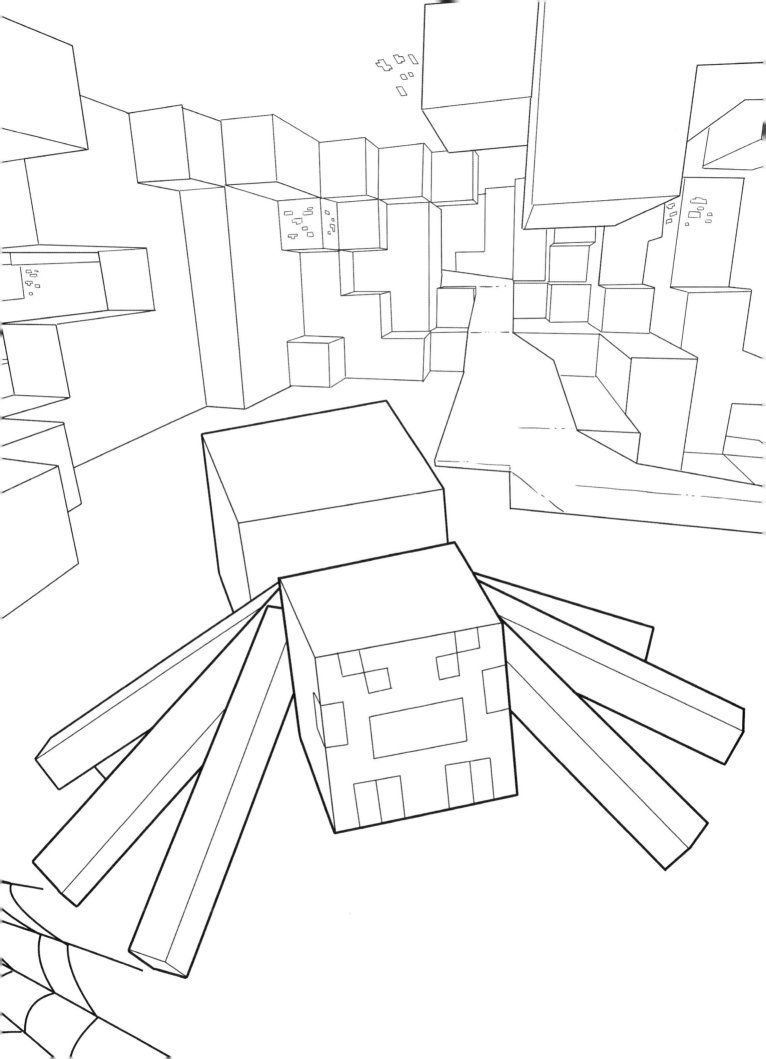

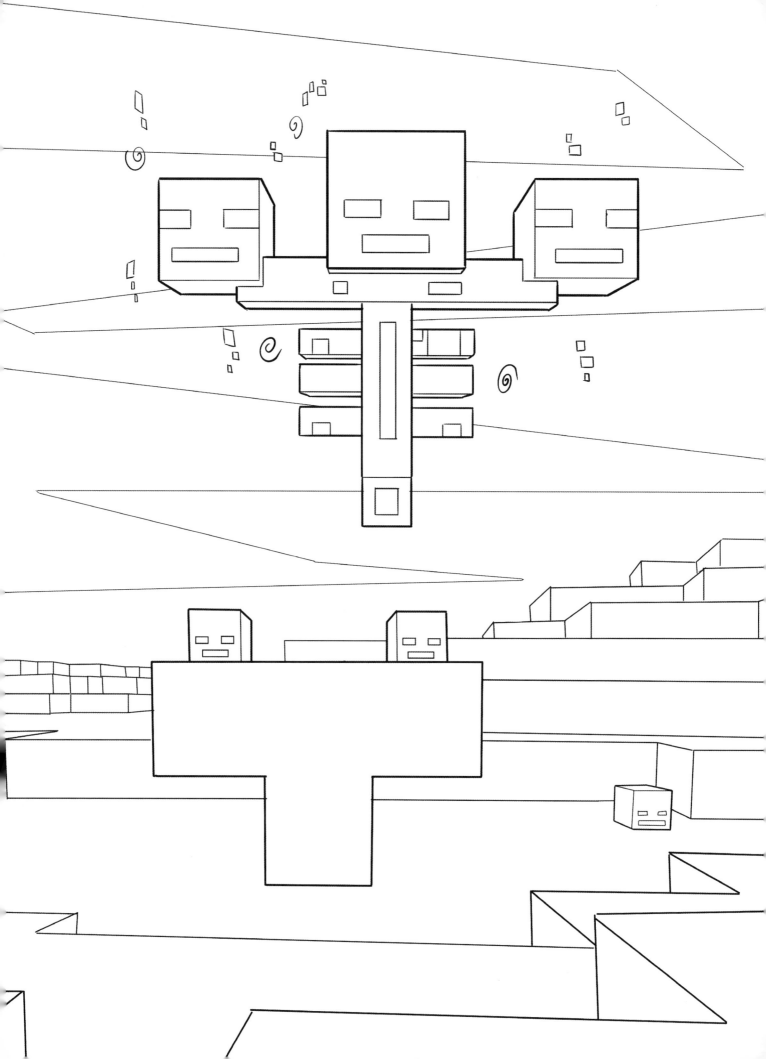

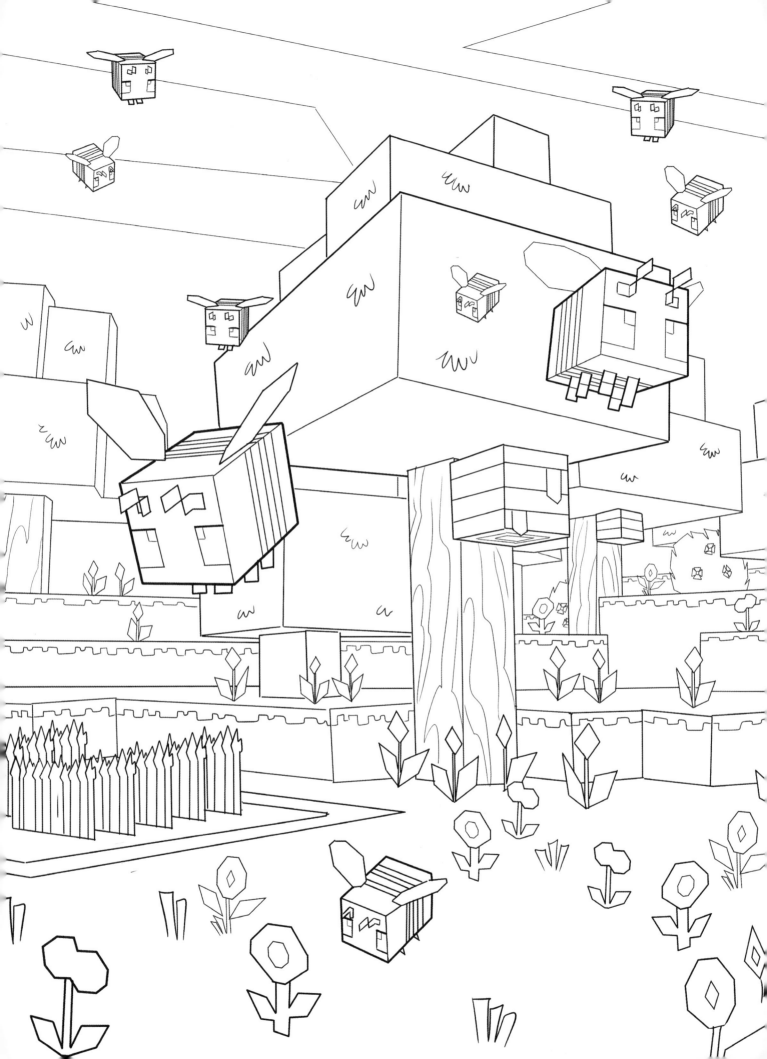

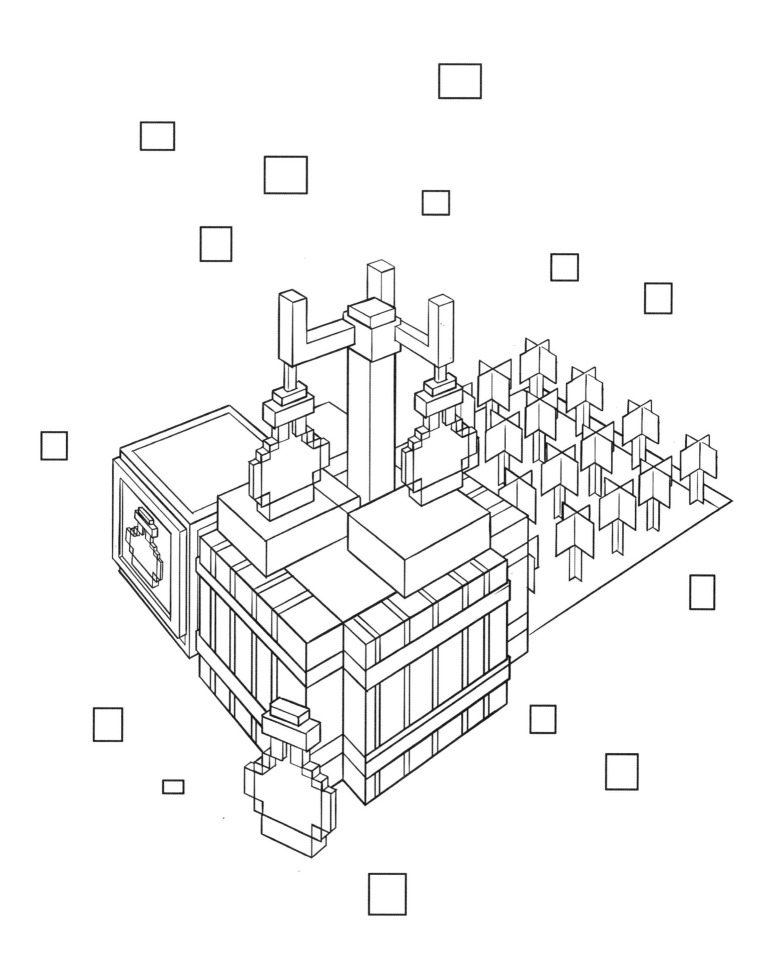

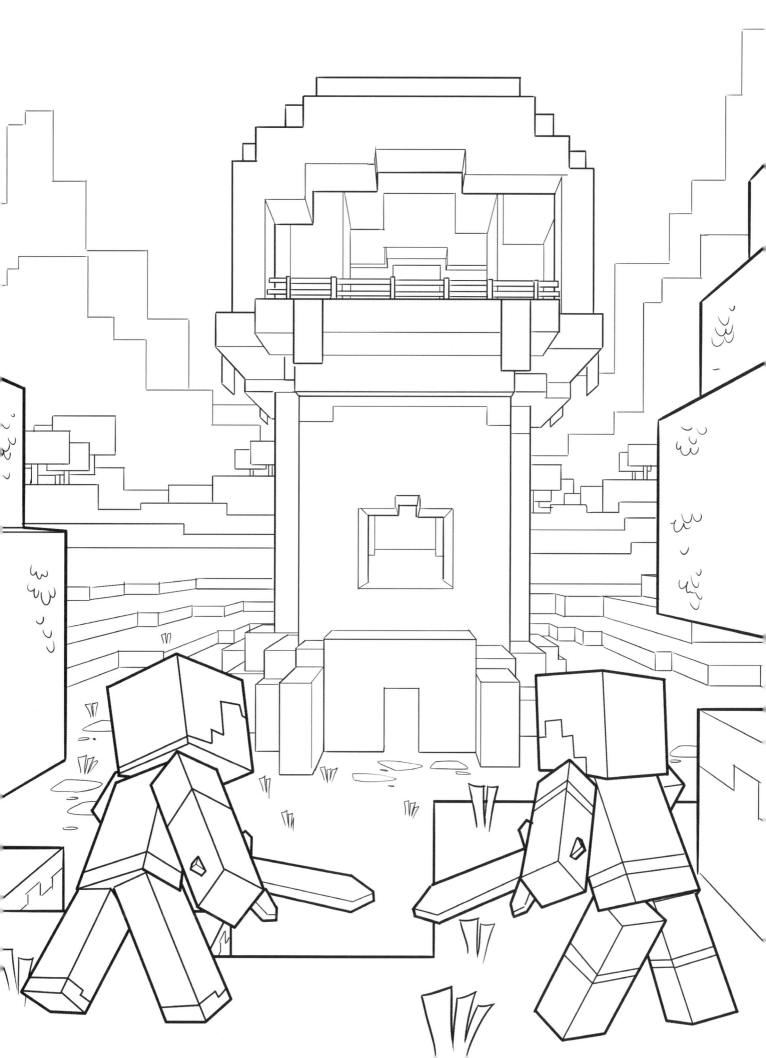

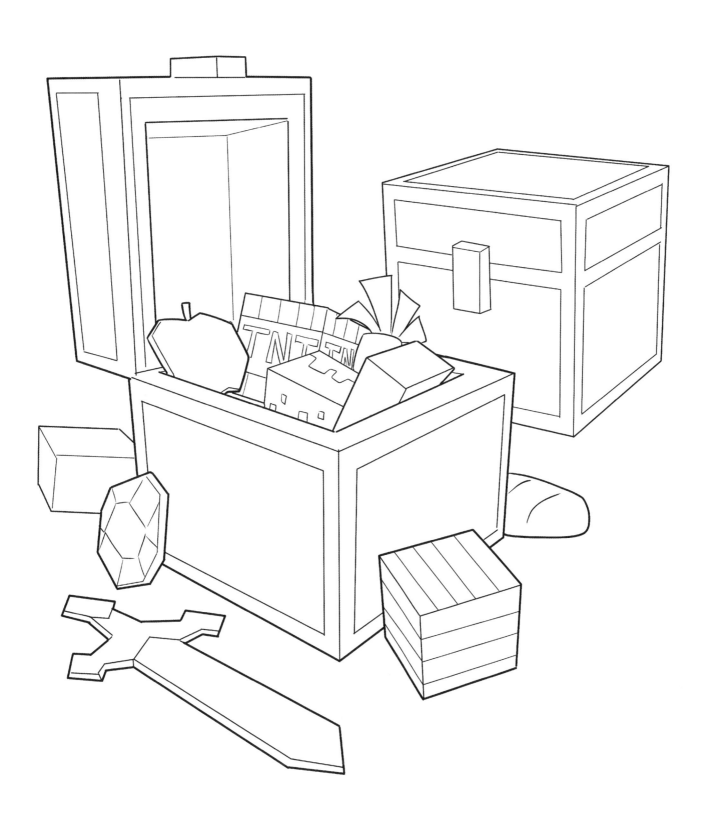

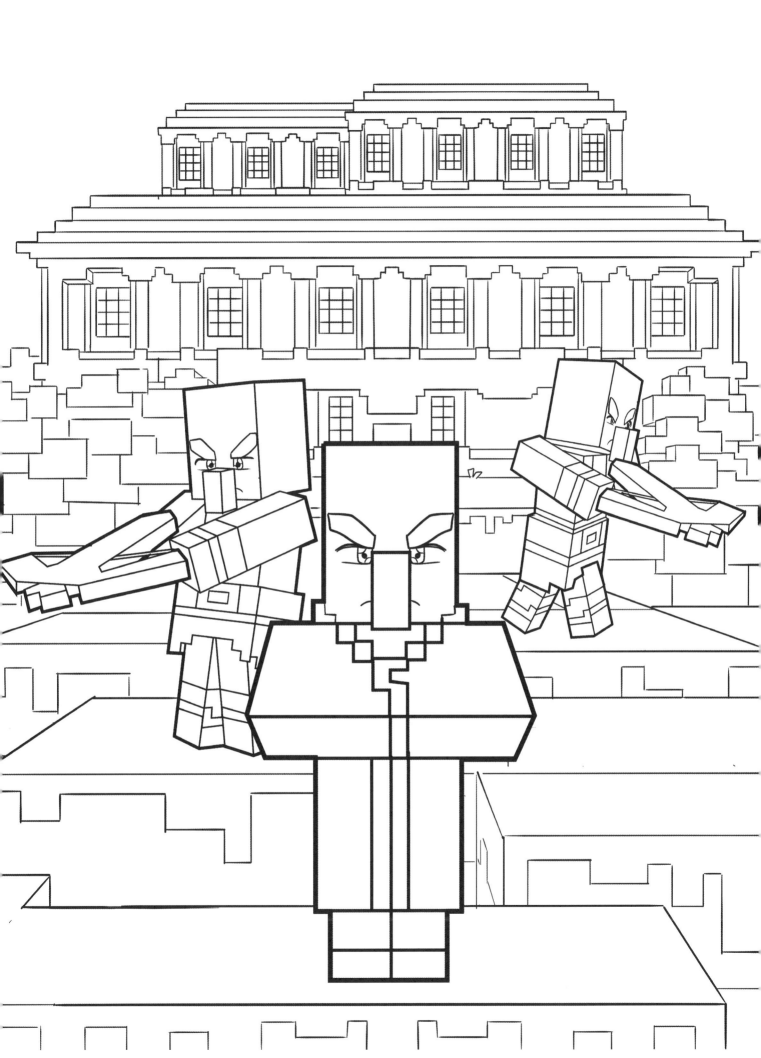

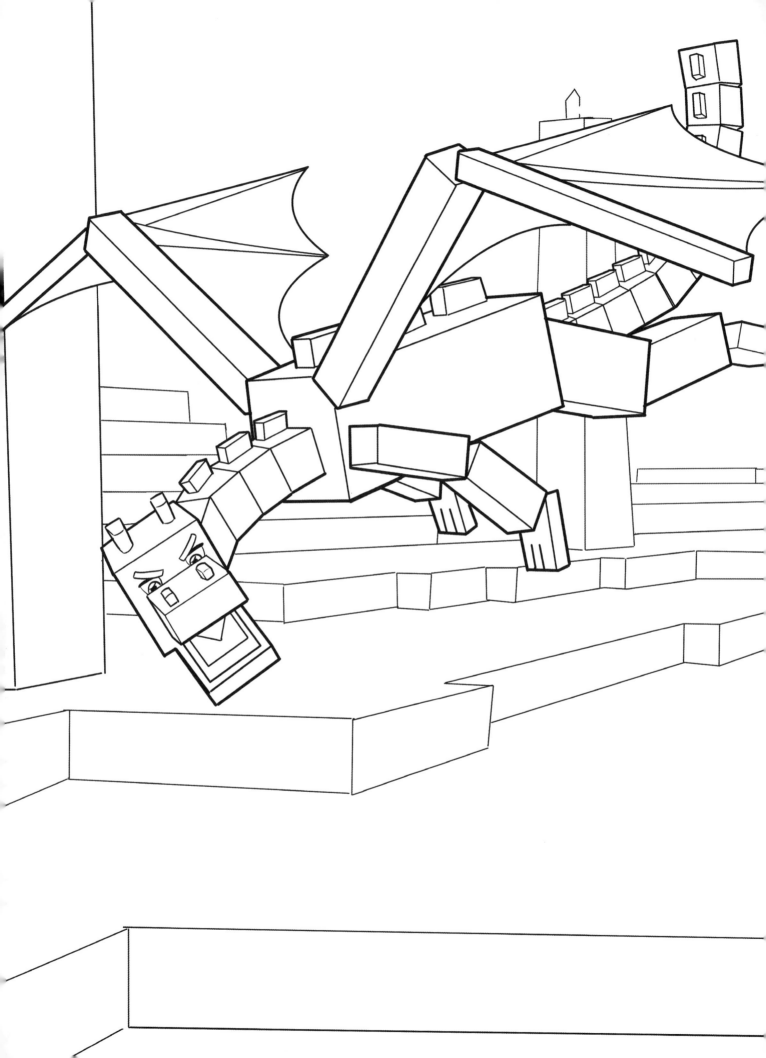

**Published by Titan Books, London, in 2022**

# TITAN BOOKS

**A division of Titan Publishing Group Ltd**

**144 Southwark Street**

**London SE1 0UP**

**www.titanbooks.com**

 Find us on Facebook: facebook.com/TitanBooks

Follow us on Twitter: @TitanBooks

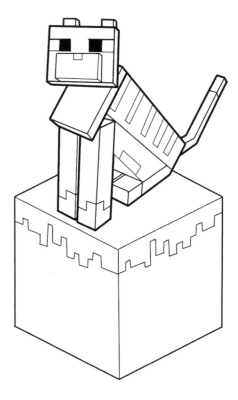

A CIP catalogue record for this title is available from the British Library.

ISBN: 978-1-80336-385-1

Published in the US by Insight Editions, San Rafael, California, in 2022.

**Publisher: Raoul Goff**

**VP of Licensing and Partnerships: Vanessa Lopez**

**VP of Creative: Chrissy Kwasnik**

**VP of Manufacturing: Alix Nicholaeff**

**Editorial Director: Vicki Jaeger**

**Design Manager: Megan Sinead Harris**

**Editor: Anna Wostenberg**

**Editorial Assistant: Harrison Tunggal**

**Production Editor: Michael Hylton**

**Production Associate: Kevin G. Yuen**

**Senior Production Manager, Subsidiary Rights: Lina s Palma**

**Special thanks to Audrey Searcy, Alex Wiltshire, Sherin Kwan, and everyone at Mojang Studios.**

Insight Editions, in association with Roots of Peace, will plant two trees for each tree used in the manufacturing of this book. Roots of Peace is an internationally renowned humanitarian organization dedicated to eradicating land mines worldwide and converting war-torn lands into productive farms and wildlife habitats. Roots of Peace will plant two million fruit and nut trees in Afghanistan and provide farmers there with the skills and support necessary for sustainable land use.

Manufactured in Turkey by Insight Editions

10 9 8 7 6 5 4 3 2 1